Inspirational

SOCCER STORIES

For

Young Readers

© **Copyright 2024 - All rights reserved.**

You may not reproduce, duplicate or send the contents of this book without direct written permission from the author. You cannot hereby despite any circumstance blame the publisher or hold him or her to legal responsibility for any reparation, compensations, or monetary forfeiture owing to the information included herein, either in a direct or an indirect way.

Legal Notice: This book has copyright protection. You can use the book for personal purposes. You should not sell, use, alter, distribute, quote, take excerpts, or paraphrase in part or whole the material contained in this book without obtaining the permission of the author first.

Disclaimer Notice: You must take note that the information in this document is for casual reading and entertainment purposes only. We have made every attempt to provide accurate, up-to-date, and reliable information. We do not express or imply guarantees of any kind. The persons who read admit that the writer is not occupied in giving legal, financial, medical, or other advice. We put this book content by sourcing various places.

Please consult a licensed professional before you try any techniques shown in this book. By going through this document, the book lover comes to an agreement that under no situation is the author accountable for any forfeiture, direct or indirect, which they may incur because of the use of material contained in this document, including, but not limited to, a errors, omissions, or inaccuracies.

Table of Contents

INTRODUCTION 5

THE KING OF FOOTBALL: PELÉ'S JOURNEY TO GLORY 7

    WHAT DID WE LEARN FROM PELÉ? 12

DIEGO MARADONA: A STORY OF FLAWED GENIUS AND UNYIELDING SPIRIT 15

    WHAT DID WE LEARN FROM DIEGO MARADONA? ... 20

LIONEL MESSI: THE JOURNEY FROM FRAGILITY TO FOOTBALL IMMORTALITY 23

    WHAT DID WE LEARN FROM LIONEL MESSI? 29

CRISTIANO RONALDO: THE JOURNEY OF PERSISTENCE AND PASSION 32

    WHAT DID WE LEARN FROM CRISTIANO RONALDO? 37

JOHAN CRUYFF: THE MASTERMIND WHO TRANSFORMED FOOTBALL 40

    WHAT DID WE LEARN FROM JOHAN CRUYFF? 45

FRANZ BECKENBAUER: THE ARCHITECT OF MODERN FOOTBALL 48

    WHAT DID WE LEARN FROM FRANZ BECKENBAUER? 53

ZINEDINE ZIDANE: MASTERY, GRACE, AND REDEMPTION ON THE GLOBAL STAGE 56

    WHAT DID WE LEARN FROM ZINEDINE ZIDANE? 61

RONALDINHO: THE SMILE OF FOOTBALL........64
    WHAT DID WE LEARN FROM RONALDINHO? 70

RONALDO NAZÁRIO: THE PHENOMENON'S TRIUMPH 73
    WHAT DID WE LEARN FROM RONALDO NAZÁRIO? 79

MICHEL PLATINI: ARTISTRY, LEADERSHIP, AND LEGACY. 83
    WHAT DID WE LEARN FROM MICHEL PLATINI? 88

GEORGE BEST: TALENT, TRIUMPH, AND TRAGEDY 92
    WHAT DID WE LEARN FROM GEORGE BEST? 97

BOBBY CHARLTON: A TALE OF TRIUMPH AND TENACITY 101
    WHAT DID WE LEARN FROM BOBBY CHARLTON? 106

ALFREDO DI STEFANO: THE BLOND ARROW WHO TRANSFORMED REAL MADRID... 110
    WHAT DID WE LEARN FROM ALFREDO DI STEFANO? 115

GERD MÜLLER: THE GOAL-SCORING MACHINE 119
    WHAT DID WE LEARN FROM GERD MÜLLER? 124

PAOLO MALDINI: A LEGACY OF EXCELLENCE AND LOYALTY 128
    WHAT DID WE LEARN FROM PAOLO MALDINI? 133

Introduction

Hey young fans! Have you ever wondered how a kid like you can become a football legend? Grab your favorite jersey and lace up your cleats as we dive into the amazing tales of the greatest football stars in history! 🎇⚽

" Inspirational Soccer Stories " is your ticket to discovering how iconic players like Messi with his magical dribbles, Ronaldo with his lightning-fast sprints, and Ronaldinho with his dazzling tricks, transformed playground dreams into stadium cheers. Each story is packed with action, challenges, and some secret moves that helped these heroes lead their teams to victory.

Imagine scoring a winning goal like Pelé, or making a game-saving tackle like Maldini.

From heart-pumping matches and incredible comebacks to learning what it takes to be a team captain, this book is your all-access pass to the exciting world of football.

Get ready to be inspired by stories that show how dedication, practice, and passion can help you kick your way from the schoolyard to the big leagues. Perfect for bedtime reading or sharing with friends, " Inspirational Soccer Stories " will make you believe in the power of dreams and perhaps start your journey to becoming a football legend yourself!

Are you ready to score big? Let's go, future champions! 🏆🚀

The King of Football: Pelé's Journey to Glory

Edson Arantes do Nascimento, known globally as Pelé, began his journey in the small Brazilian town of Três Corações. Born in 1940 into modest circumstances, young Pelé grew up shining shoes to help his family make ends meet. Despite the financial hardships, Pelé's early life was rich in one invaluable asset—his love for football. This passion saw him kicking a rolled-up sock stuffed with rags, dreaming of a future far beyond the streets of his hometown.

Pelé's raw talent was undeniable, and by the age of 15, he was playing for Santos FC. His impact was immediate and profound. With dazzling footwork and an uncanny ability to score, Pelé led Santos to numerous state and national championships. His signature move, the "Pelé runaround," where he would deceive the goalkeeper by not touching the ball, became legendary.

The world first witnessed Pelé's brilliance at the 1958 FIFA World Cup in Sweden. At just 17 years old, he was the youngest player in the tournament. Pelé's performance was nothing short of miraculous, as he scored a hat-trick in the semifinals against France and two more goals in the finals against Sweden. Brazil lifted the World Cup, and Pelé wept openly with joy—a teenager at the pinnacle of the footballing world.

Pelé's influence extended beyond his club and country. He became a symbol of hope and pride for Brazilians, uniting a nation plagued by political instability and economic challenges. His style of play brought joy and beauty to a sport that transcended the boundaries of language and culture, earning him the title "The King of Football."

Despite his skyrocketing fame, Pelé faced challenges both on and off the field. He endured brutal fouls from opponents and immense pressure to perform at every game. Yet, his commitment never wavered. Pelé's presence at the 1962 and 1970 World Cups further cemented his legacy, helping Brazil to claim two more world titles. His performance in the 1970 tournament in Mexico, where he showcased his mature mastery of the game, is still considered one of the finest in the history of football.

Off the field, Pelé used his fame to advocate for social change and development in Brazil and beyond. He worked tirelessly to promote sports and education among the youth, understanding his role as a model for future generations. Even after his retirement in 1977, Pelé continued to be an ambassador for football, representing the sport in various capacities on the global stage.

Pelé's story is not just about his world-class talent or his three World Cup titles. It is about a boy who transformed his life and inspired millions by following his passion and believing in his dreams. His legacy teaches us that with talent, determination, and heart, it's possible to overcome any obstacle and achieve greatness.

Pelé remains not just a testament to the power of sports but a beacon of hope, demonstrating that greatness starts with a dream and a relentless spirit to pursue it.

What Did We Learn from Pelé?

Pelé's legacy transcends the boundaries of sport, teaching us profound lessons about passion, perseverance, and the power of dreams. From the humble streets of Três Corações to the global stage, Pelé's journey exemplifies how dedication and hard work can transform innate talent into legendary achievement.

We learned that resilience can overcome any obstacle. Despite the hardships of his early life and the physical challenges he faced on the pitch, Pelé's unyielding spirit never faltered. His ability to rise above adversity, whether in the form of poverty or aggressive play by opponents, underscores the importance of mental toughness and determination.

Pelé also taught us the value of grace and humility. Amidst unparalleled success and worldwide fame, he remained grounded and consistently used his platform to uplift others. His commitment to social change and the development of youth through sports and education shows that true greatness involves giving back and empowering the next generation.

Moreover, Pelé embodied the joy of soccer, reminding us that at the heart of every endeavor, love and passion are paramount. He played with a smile, celebrating each goal not as a personal triumph but as a communal joy. This attitude not only endeared him to millions but also revolutionized the way the sport is played and appreciated.

Ultimately, Pelé's story encourages us all to dream big and to pursue those dreams with all our hearts. It teaches us that the path to greatness is paved with persistence, humility, and an unwavering love for what we do. Pelé was not just a footballer; he was a beacon of hope and a testament to the idea that with talent, dedication, and heart, anyone can overcome the odds and achieve greatness. His legacy will forever inspire not only athletes but all who strive to make their dreams a reality.

Diego Maradona: A Story of Flawed Genius and Unyielding Spirit

In the bustling streets of Villa Fiorito, a poor neighborhood in Buenos Aires, a young boy named Diego Armando Maradona discovered his destiny. Born on October 30, 1960, into a family that struggled to make ends meet, Maradona found solace and expression in a soccer ball. His early life was marked by hardship, but also by a profound love for football, which served both as a playground and a potential escape from poverty.

Maradona's exceptional talent became evident when he joined Los Cebollitas, a youth team of Argentinos Juniors, at the age of 10. His skill was so advanced that he often played with much older players, dazzling spectators with his dribbling. Even then, his coach said, "He was born with a gift." Diego's gift wasn't just his ability to control the ball, but to inspire those around him with his sheer determination and joy for the game.

At 16, Maradona made his professional debut for Argentinos Juniors, and from there, his career trajectory was meteoric. By 1982, he had moved to Barcelona and then to Napoli in 1984, where his impact would be nothing short of legendary. In Naples, Maradona was more than just a football player; he was a symbol of hope for a city that often felt forgotten by the rest of Italy. His arrival brought a sense of pride to the local people, and his success on the pitch brought them unparalleled joy.

Maradona led Napoli to their first-ever Serie A Italian Championship in 1987, followed by another in 1990. His presence transformed the club and the city, knitting his name into the fabric of Napoli's identity. However, it was his performance in the 1986 World Cup for Argentina that defined his career. In this tournament, Maradona executed what would become known as the 'Hand of God' goal and the 'Goal of the Century' against England—moments of controversy and brilliance that underscored his complex persona.

Off the field, Maradona faced numerous challenges, including battles with substance abuse and health issues, which often played out in the public eye. His life was a rollercoaster of spectacular highs and devastating lows, mirroring the dribbles he was famous for on the field. Yet, despite his struggles, Maradona's influence on football remained undiminished.

Maradona retired in 1997, leaving behind a legacy complicated by his imperfections but he was also celebrated for his extraordinary contributions to football. He was not only a genius on the field but also a man who showed that human frailty and greatness could coexist. His death on November 25, 2020, prompted an outpouring of tributes worldwide, not just for the player he was, but for the indomitable spirit he embodied.

Diego Maradona's story is a testament to the transformative power of sport. It tells us that heroes are not born from perfection but from the ability to overcome, inspire, and leave an indelible mark on the world and the people around them, despite and often because of their flaws.

What Did We Learn from Diego Maradona?

Diego Maradona's journey through the world of football is not just a tale of athletic prowess but also a story of pure passion and the complexities of fame. From the humble barrios of Buenos Aires to becoming a global icon, Maradona's life teaches us about the raw power of determination and the double-edged sword of extraordinary talent.

We learned that genius comes with its challenges. Maradona's magical abilities on the field, marked by the infamous "Hand of God" and his mesmerizing solo goal against England in the 1986 World Cup, demonstrated his unparalleled skill and audacity. However, his life off the pitch showed us that even the most gifted individuals face personal battles, and that talent can both elevate and isolate.

Maradona also taught us about resilience. Through every high and low, he displayed an incredible capacity to rebound and reinvent himself. Whether facing fierce criticism, battling health issues, or dealing with controversies, Maradona's resilience in the face of adversity was as profound as his creativity with the ball at his feet.

Moreover, Maradona's life reminds us of the power of authenticity. He was unapologetically passionate and wore his heart on his sleeve, embodying the spirit of Argentina. His deep connection with his roots and his raw emotional expression on and off the field resonated deeply with fans, making him not just a player but a beloved national hero.

From Maradona, we learn that greatness is multifaceted. It involves not only moments of brilliance but also enduring the pressures that come with them. His legacy is a testament to the idea that while our talents can elevate us, our struggles and how we navigate them define our true character. Maradona's story is a powerful reminder that by embracing our humanity, with all its flaws and virtues, we can touch the hearts of millions and become unforgettable legends in our own right.

Lionel Messi: The Journey from Fragility to Football Immortality

In the modest town of Rosario, Argentina, Lionel Messi was born on June 24, 1987, into a working-class family. From a young age, it was clear that Messi had an extraordinary talent for football, but his journey to the top was not without significant challenges.

At the tender age of 11, Messi was diagnosed with a growth hormone deficiency. The treatment was costly, and while his local club, Newell's Old Boys, initially agreed to contribute, the economic crisis in Argentina soon made it impossible for them to support his medical needs. Despite this setback, Messi's passion and skill were undeniable, leading his family to make a life-changing decision. His father, Jorge, secured a trial with FC Barcelona, and the club was so impressed with Messi's abilities that they offered to pay for his medical treatments.

The move to Barcelona at 13 was daunting; Messi spoke little Spanish, distinct from his native Argentine dialect, and he was thousands of miles away from home. He struggled with homesickness and adaptation to a new culture. However, his determination to play the sport he loved saw him through these tough times. His talent quickly shone through, and by the age of 17, Messi made his official debut for the first team, setting the stage for one of the most illustrious careers in football history.

Messi's impact on the world stage was immediate. His playing style, characterized by his low center of gravity, incredible close control, and a seemingly telepathic understanding of the game, drew comparisons to football legend Diego Maradona. Over the years, Messi developed an iconic rivalry with Cristiano Ronaldo, another contender for the title of the greatest player of all time, which thrilled fans worldwide.

Throughout his career at Barcelona, Messi shattered records, including the most goals in a calendar year and the most hat-tricks in La Liga. His accolades include multiple FIFA Ballon d'Or awards, and he led Barcelona to numerous titles, including four Champions League trophies. Messi's leadership on the pitch and his humility off it endeared him to fans and fellow players alike.

One of the most defining moments of his career came during the 2014 World Cup. Despite Argentina not winning the tournament, Messi's performance earned him the Golden Ball as the tournament's best player. His emotional resilience shone brightly in 2021 when he led Argentina to victory in the Copa America, his first major international trophy, which solidified his status as a national hero.

Off the field, Messi has utilized his fame to support various charitable efforts, particularly those improving children's health and education worldwide. His involvement with UNICEF and his charitable organization, the Leo Messi Foundation, highlights his commitment to giving back to the community.

   Lionel Messi's story is not just about his supernatural abilities on the football field; it is a narrative of overcoming adversity, maintaining resilience in the face of personal and professional challenges, and remaining humble despite global fame. His journey from a fragile boy in Rosario to a footballing legend is a testament to the power of dedication, proving that with passion and perseverance, any obstacle can be overcome.

What Did We Learn from Lionel Messi?

Lionel Messi's illustrious career, marked by astonishing skill and unparalleled success, offers a blueprint of what can be achieved through sheer dedication and love for one's craft. From his early days at Barcelona's famed La Masia to dominating the world stage, Messi's journey is a testament to the power of commitment and the importance of staying true to one's roots.

We learned from Messi that greatness is often silent; it does not always shout but rather demonstrates itself through consistent action. His humility on and off the pitch, despite being one of the greatest footballers of all time, reminds us that true champions do not need to boast about their achievements. They let their work speak for itself.

Messi's career also teaches us about overcoming adversity. Diagnosed with a growth hormone deficiency as a child, he faced a significant hurdle that could have ended his football dreams. However, his resolve to succeed and his family's sacrifices to provide treatment exemplified that obstacles are just stepping stones on the path to success.

Moreover, Messi shows the value of focused passion. His mesmerizing dribbling, exceptional vision, and scoring ability did not come solely from innate talent but from countless hours of practice and an unwavering dedication to improving every aspect of his game. This teaches us that to excel in any field, passion must be paired with discipline and hard work.

From Lionel Messi, we learn that humility, resilience, and dedication are as important as natural talent. His career is a powerful narrative that encourages us to pursue our passions relentlessly, handle success with grace, and never forget where we came from, no matter the heights we reach. Messi's legacy inspires us not only to dream but to work tirelessly towards turning those dreams into reality.

Cristiano Ronaldo: The Journey of Persistence and Passion

Cristiano Ronaldo's story is a quintessential tale of aspiration, resilience, and undying belief in one's own abilities. Born in 1985 in Madeira, Portugal, Ronaldo grew up in a small, rustic home, far from the glittering lights of international football stadiums. The youngest child of a cook and a gardener, he shared a room with his siblings and faced many hardships that could have easily diverted his path away from his dreams.

From a very young age, Ronaldo displayed a fierce passion for football, spending every possible moment playing, often skipping meals or escaping out of windows to practice. His talent was undeniable, and by the age of 12, he had already made a name for himself on the local scene, enough to warrant a move to Sporting Lisbon's academy, over 600 miles away from his family.

The transition was challenging for young Ronaldo. He was far from home, surrounded by strangers, and often found himself ridiculed for his Madeiran accent. However, rather than deterring him, these challenges fueled his determination. He practiced relentlessly, honed his skills, and rapidly progressed through the youth ranks, driven by a relentless pursuit of greatness.

Ronaldo's breakthrough came at 16 when he played against Manchester United while at Sporting. His performance was so outstanding that it not only helped his team win but also impressed the opposing team's players and manager so much that they urged their club to sign him. Shortly after, he joined Manchester United, marking the start of an illustrious career that would see him rise to the pinnacle of global football.

At Manchester United, and later at Real Madrid and Juventus, Ronaldo's career flourished. His work ethic was legendary; he was the first to arrive at training and the last to leave, constantly striving to improve his speed, strength, and skills. His ability to perform under pressure, his knack for decisive goals in crucial games, and his fitness regimen became hallmarks of his career, inspiring teammates and rivals alike.

Off the field, Ronaldo faced personal and professional challenges, including public scrutiny and personal tragedies like the loss of his father. However, he consistently used these experiences to fuel his motivation rather than as an excuse for faltering. His dedication to his family, particularly his mother and children, kept him grounded and focused.

Today, Ronaldo is not just a football legend but a global icon of dedication and success against all odds. His life teaches us the power of resilience and hard work. Ronaldo's journey shows that no matter where you come from, your dreams are valid and achievable with persistence and faith in yourself. It's a testament to the belief that talent is important, but the will to prepare and persevere is what truly makes one a champion.

What Did We Learn from Cristiano Ronaldo?

Cristiano Ronaldo's remarkable journey from the modest neighborhoods of Madeira to the summit of international football encapsulates invaluable lessons about ambition, discipline, and resilience.

From him, we learned the power of self-belief. Ronaldo's unwavering confidence in his abilities, even when faced with skepticism or outright criticism, teaches us the importance of trusting in our potential. His attitude demonstrates that believing in oneself is the first step toward achieving greatness.

Ronaldo also exemplified the virtue of hard work. Known for his meticulous training regimen and dedication, he embodies the adage that talent without hard work is nothing. His relentless drive to improve, to push his limits further each day, serves as a vivid reminder that success is not given but earned through persistent effort and determination.

Moreover, Ronaldo's career highlights the significance of resilience. Facing numerous challenges, both on and off the field—from his humble beginnings and early career injuries to personal losses—he has shown that setbacks can be stepping stones to success if faced with courage and perseverance.

Additionally, Ronaldo teaches us about the impact of professionalism and leadership. Throughout his career, he has set standards in professionalism, maintaining his physique and skill level through rigorous training and diet. His ability to inspire and lead his teammates, whether at the club or national level, underscores the role of a leader in elevating everyone around them to achieve common goals.

Ultimately, Cristiano Ronaldo's story is a testament to the fact that our background does not define us; our actions do. It's a powerful narrative that encourages us to chase our dreams with hard work, discipline, and a never-give-up attitude, making him not just a sports icon, but a global symbol of hope and inspiration.

Johan Cruyff: The Mastermind Who Transformed Football

Johan Cruyff's story is one of innovation, influence, and indomitable spirit, both on and off the football field. Born in 1947 in Amsterdam, Cruyff's connection with football began at an early age, growing up near the stadium of AFC Ajax. His football journey started with Ajax, where he quickly progressed through the ranks due to his evident talent and understanding of the game.

Cruyff's playing style was revolutionary. Known for his agility, speed, and intelligence, he became the embodiment of "Total Football," a tactic where players dynamically swapped positions, allowing the team to maintain its structure regardless of the play. This style not only captivated spectators but also redefined strategies in European football.

His impact at Ajax was profound, leading the club to multiple Dutch championships and three consecutive European Cups from 1971 to 1973. His performances earned him the Ballon d'Or three times during his career, marking him as the best player in the world.

In 1973, Cruyff moved to Barcelona, a club then in the shadows of its rivals. His arrival marked a turning point for the Catalan club. Under his influence, Barcelona won La Liga for the first time in 14 years. But Cruyff's contribution went beyond his skills on the pitch; his vision for the club's future began shaping what would become the modern Barcelona, emphasizing youth development and a style of play that focused on skill over strength.

Cruyff's philosophy extended to his managerial career, where he had an equally transformative impact. Returning to Ajax and later moving to Barcelona as a manager, he instilled the principles of Total Football and laid the groundwork for the future success of both clubs. At Barcelona, he formed the "Dream Team," which won four consecutive La Liga titles and the club's first European Cup in 1992.

Off the field, Cruyff was known for his outspoken nature and intellectual approach to the game. He was a mentor to future stars and coaches, including Pep Guardiola, who would carry forward his football philosophy to achieve new heights.

His legacy, however, extends beyond trophies and accolades. Cruyff used his prominence to influence positive changes, founding the Johan Cruyff Foundation, which focuses on enabling children to engage in sports and improve their fitness, teamwork, and social integration through sport.

Johan Cruyff's story teaches us that vision and passion can change not just games but lives. His innovations reshaped modern football, and his commitment to development and education showed that the true value of sport lies in its power to inspire and unite. Cruyff not only changed how football is played but also how it is perceived, making him a true legend of the game.

What Did We Learn from Johan Cruyff?

Johan Cruyff's profound impact on football offers enduring lessons about creativity, leadership, and the transformative power of ideas. From his days as a visionary player to his time as an influential coach and thinker, Cruyff taught us the importance of seeing beyond the conventional.

From him, we learned the significance of innovation in any field. Cruyff was not just a football participant; he was a pioneer who rethought the way the game was played and coached. His concept of Total Football—a fluid, interchangeable style where every player could adapt and thrive in multiple positions—revolutionized football tactics. This teaches us that challenging the status quo can lead to groundbreaking advancements.

Cruyff also exemplified the value of intellectual courage. He was never afraid to voice his opinions or to stand up for his principles, whether critiquing an established practice or advocating for youth involvement in sports. His boldness in expressing and acting on his beliefs reminds us that true leadership often requires standing alone and having the courage to lead change.

Moreover, his approach to coaching highlighted the importance of empowerment. Cruyff believed in the potential of his players, encouraging them to think independently and play with freedom. This method fostered not only better players but also future leaders who carried forward his philosophy. It underscores the lesson that empowering others can amplify our impact and leave a lasting legacy.

Finally, Johan Cruyff taught us about the power of sport as a tool for social good. Through his foundation, he demonstrated how sports could be a vehicle for social change, improving children's lives by promoting physical and mental health, teamwork, and social integration.

In essence, Johan Cruyff's life and career show us that it's possible to leave a meaningful and lasting impact with innovative thinking, courageous leadership, and a commitment to empowering others. His legacy in football and beyond serves as a powerful reminder of how one person's vision can alter landscapes and inspire generations.

Franz Beckenbauer: The Architect of Modern Football

Franz Beckenbauer's journey from the streets of post-war Munich to becoming one of football's greatest legends is a story of vision, leadership, and resilience. Known affectionately as "Der Kaiser" for his commanding presence on and off the field, Beckenbauer redefined the role of a defender, transforming it into a position of grace, intelligence, and authority.

Born in 1945, Beckenbauer grew up in a Germany still reeling from the effects of World War II. Football provided a much-needed escape from the hardships of daily life. His natural talent was evident from an early age, and by the time he was 14, he had joined Bayern Munich, a club that would become synonymous with his name.

Beckenbauer's playing style was revolutionary. Before him, defenders were typically the bulwark of the team, focused primarily on stopping attacks. Beckenbauer, however, saw an opportunity to add creativity to this role. He became known for his ability to read the game, making incisive passes and often venturing forward to support the attack, effectively creating the role of the modern sweeper or libero.

Under his leadership, both as a captain and central figure, Bayern Munich rose to dominance in the 1970s, claiming three consecutive European Cups from 1974 to 1976. His elegance on the ball, strategic insight, and defensive prowess set new standards in football.

Beckenbauer's international career with West Germany was equally illustrious. He earned his first cap at just 20 years old and soon became captain. His defining moment came in the 1974 World Cup held in West Germany. Despite suffering a painful shoulder injury in the second game of the tournament, Beckenbauer refused to quit. With his arm in a sling, he continued to play, leading his team with remarkable courage and determination. His resilience and leadership culminated in West Germany winning the World Cup, a triumph that became a symbol of recovery and pride for his country.

After retiring as a player, Beckenbauer seamlessly transitioned to management, leading West Germany to victory in the 1990 World Cup in Italy. This achievement made him one of the few individuals to have won the Cup both as a player and as a coach, cementing his legacy as a footballing great.

Beyond the pitch, Beckenbauer has been instrumental in promoting football across the globe. His charisma and respected voice have made him a popular ambassador for the sport, and he is involved in various initiatives to develop football worldwide.

Franz Beckenbauer's story teaches us the power of innovation and leadership in achieving greatness. His life reminds us that the roles we play can be redefined and that leadership is not just about commanding presence, but about resilience, vision, and the courage to lead by example. Beckenbauer's legacy is a testament to the idea that with enough creativity and determination, one can leave a lasting imprint not just on a sport, but on the entire world.

What Did We Learn from Franz Beckenbauer?

Franz Beckenbauer, known as "Der Kaiser," left an indelible mark on football, teaching us invaluable lessons about innovation, leadership, and the power of resilience.

From Beckenbauer, we learned the importance of redefining roles. He transformed the position of the sweeper (libero) from a purely defensive role into one that is also creative and strategic. Beckenbauer showed that with vision and skill, traditional roles can be reinterpreted to enhance a team's dynamics and success. This lesson extends beyond sports, encouraging us in any field to think innovatively and push the boundaries of conventional roles.

His leadership on and off the field teaches us about the essence of leading by example. Beckenbauer's calm demeanor under pressure, strategic thinking, and ability to inspire his teammates were central to his teams' successes at both club and international levels. He demonstrated that true leaders do not merely instruct but lead through action, setting standards for others to follow.

Beckenbauer's resilience, particularly evident during the 1974 World Cup where he played with a severe shoulder injury, highlights his strength of character and determination. His ability to endure pain and lead his team to victory exemplifies the kind of grit and perseverance required to overcome challenges and achieve goals, no matter the obstacles.

Moreover, his transition from a world-class player to a successful coach illustrates the value of adaptability and lifelong learning. Beckenbauer seamlessly moved into coaching, applying his deep understanding of the game to lead Germany to another World Cup victory in 1990. This aspect of his career shows that continual growth and adaptation are crucial for sustained success.

From Franz Beckenbauer, we learn that innovation, leadership, resilience, and adaptability are not just traits but choices that one can cultivate to excel and leave a lasting legacy. His life and career are a testament to the power of these qualities in achieving greatness and influencing others positively.

Zinedine Zidane: Mastery, Grace, and Redemption on the Global Stage

Zinedine Zidane's story is one of elegance on the football pitch, and of a journey marked by both extraordinary highs and challenging lows, culminating in a tale of redemption and lasting legacy. Born in 1972 in Marseille, France, to Algerian immigrants, Zidane grew up in the tough neighborhood of La Castellane. His early life was filled with challenges, but football offered a path to a different life, a way to express himself and transcend his circumstances.

From the streets of Marseille to the grand stadiums of the world, Zidane's talent was undeniable. His first significant breakthrough came when he joined Bordeaux in the French league, where his performances caught the attention of Europe's elite clubs. He moved to Juventus in 1996, where his skill, vision, and unique style of play flourished. Zidane's ability to control the game, paired with his iconic pirouettes and flawless ball control, earned him international acclaim.

In 1998, Zidane's career reached a new height during the FIFA World Cup held in France. In a final against Brazil, Zidane scored two crucial headers, leading France to its first World Cup victory. This triumph made him a national hero, an emblem of both French and multicultural success. Zidane's performance in the World Cup showcased his ability to rise to the occasion, reflecting his resilience and mental fortitude.

Zidane's journey was not without its trials. His career saw moments of controversy, including a notorious red card in the 2006 World Cup final—his last professional match—when he headbutted an Italian player. This incident could have overshadowed his contributions, but Zidane's response in later years, focusing on coaching and philanthropy, helped reshape his narrative.

After retiring as a player, Zidane transitioned into coaching, taking the helm at Real Madrid. His tenure as a coach was marked by remarkable success, including winning three consecutive UEFA Champions League titles, a feat that solidified his legacy as one of football's great minds. Zidane demonstrated that his football intelligence and leadership extended beyond playing, highlighting his adaptability and strategic acumen.

Off the field, Zidane has been a fervent advocate for charitable causes, using his status to promote education and health for disadvantaged children around the world. His ongoing commitment to social issues shows his understanding of the broader impact of sports figures.

Zinedine Zidane's story teaches us about the power of grace under pressure, the importance of redemption, and the impact of using one's platform for the greater good. His journey is a compelling narrative of overcoming adversity, showcasing not just the heights one can achieve with talent and hard work, but also the importance of character in defining true success. Zidane remains a figure of inspiration, proving that true legends are made by how they handle their moments of challenge as much as their moments of triumph.

What Did We Learn from Zinedine Zidane?

Zinedine Zidane's illustrious career in football, both as a player and as a coach, has imparted significant lessons about grace, mastery, and the importance of resilience.

From Zidane, we learned the art of composure and elegance under pressure. His playing style, characterized by a rare blend of finesse, balance, and spatial awareness, exemplified how poise can coexist with power on the sports field. This teaches us that true strength often resides in the ability to remain calm and collected in the face of challenges.

His career also highlighted the importance of redemption and self-improvement. Zidane's infamous headbutt in the 2006 World Cup final could have marred his legacy, but his response to this incident taught us about accountability and the power of turning a moment of failure into an opportunity for personal growth. As a coach, he further demonstrated this by leading Real Madrid to consecutive Champions League victories, showing that past mistakes do not define the future.

Moreover, Zidane's journey from the modest neighborhood of La Castellane to the pinnacle of global football underscores the value of determination and hard work. It reminds us that no matter one's background, with dedication and passion, it is possible to rise to the top of one's field.

Zidane also taught us about the significance of tactical intelligence, both on and off the field. As a player, his understanding of the game made him one of the best playmakers in football history, while as a coach, his strategic insights brought great success to his teams. This dual aspect of his career encourages us to continually learn and adapt, applying our knowledge creatively to overcome obstacles and achieve our goals.

From Zinedine Zidane, we learn that grace, accountability, continuous learning, and strategic thinking are qualities that not only define great leaders but also contribute to lasting success and respect. His legacy is a testament to the impact that one individual can have through a combination of personal excellence and a commitment to higher standards.

Ronaldinho: The Smile of Football

Ronaldo de Assis Moreira, known worldwide as Ronaldinho, embodies the joy and artistry of football like few others in the history of the sport. Born in 1980 in Porto Alegre, Brazil, Ronaldinho's path to becoming an international football icon was paved with flair, charisma, and an infectious smile that captured the hearts of fans around the globe.

Ronaldinho grew up in a family deeply passionate about football; his father was a shipyard worker and amateur footballer, and his brother was a professional footballer. Tragedy struck early when Ronaldinho was only eight; his father suffered a fatal heart attack in the family swimming pool. Despite the hardship, Ronaldinho's love for the game grew, driven by the joy it brought him and the memories of playing with his father.

His talent was evident from a young age. By the time he was 13, Ronaldinho had scored an incredible 23 goals in a single game, a feat that put him on the map. His rise through the ranks of local clubs led him to Grêmio, where he began his professional career. His breakthrough came during the 1997 U-17 World Championship, where he was recognized as the tournament's best player. His playmaking ability, exceptional dribbling skills, and no-look passes became his trademarks.

Ronaldinho's career took a significant leap forward when he moved to Europe, joining Paris Saint-Germain and later moving to

Barcelona. It was at Barcelona where Ronaldinho's skills fully blossomed. Under his influence, Barcelona transformed into one of the most spectacular teams in the world. His tenure at the club included numerous trophies, and his performances were a blend of spectacle and effectiveness, highlighted by standing ovations from rival fans and countless accolades, including the prestigious Ballon d'Or in 2005.

Beyond his club achievements, Ronaldinho was also a key player for the Brazilian national team, helping them win the 2002 FIFA World Cup. His no-look passes, behind-the-leg dribbles, and free-kicks charmed fans and perplexed opponents, making him a symbol of the sport's beauty and unpredictability.

After his peak years, Ronaldinho's career experienced ups and downs, with stints at various clubs around the world. Despite this, he remained a beloved figure in the sport, celebrated for his creative play and the sheer joy he brought to the pitch. Ronaldinho's infectious enthusiasm reminded everyone that football, at its heart, is a game meant to bring joy and unite people across different cultures and backgrounds.

Off the field, Ronaldinho has been involved in numerous charitable efforts, particularly focusing on improving the lives of children in Brazil through football. His post-retirement life has been as colorful and eventful as his career, maintaining his status as a beloved global ambassador for football.

Ronaldinho's legacy teaches us that while skill and victory are celebrated, the joy we bring to our pursuits and the happiness we share with others is just as important. His career is a testament to the power of sports to inspire, entertain, and bring people together, making him not just a player, but a true legend of the game.

What Did We Learn from Ronaldinho?

Ronaldinho's storied career offers profound lessons on passion, creativity, and the transformative power of sports. Known for his dazzling skills and magnetic personality, he demonstrated that success and joy can coexist beautifully on the global stage.

From Ronaldinho, we learned the importance of playing with joy. His ever-present smile and playful style on the field reminded everyone that at its core, football is a game meant to be enjoyed. This approach not only endeared him to fans worldwide but also showed that bringing positivity to one's work can elevate performance and inspire those around you.

Creativity and innovation were hallmarks of Ronaldinho's play. He was never afraid to try new moves, whether it was a flip-flap or a no-look pass, teaching us the value of creativity in overcoming challenges and standing out in any field. His ability to see and execute plays that others couldn't imagine reminds us that thinking outside the box can lead to extraordinary results.

Ronaldinho also exemplified resilience. Despite personal tragedies and professional setbacks, including the early loss of his father and career fluctuations, he maintained his joyful approach to the game and life. His resilience teaches us that hardships can be faced with a positive spirit and that maintaining one's essence is crucial through all of life's ups and downs.

Moreover, Ronaldinho's impact extended beyond the pitch. His involvement in charitable activities, particularly those aimed at improving the lives of children through sports, highlighted the role of athletes as global citizens who can leverage their fame for good. It underscores the lesson that success comes with the responsibility to give back and uplift others.

From Ronaldinho, we learn that while talent can make you a star, joy, creativity, resilience, and a commitment to making a positive impact can make you a legend. His legacy is not just about the goals scored or the matches won, but about inspiring people to bring passion and happiness to whatever they do.

Ronaldo Nazário: The Phenomenon's Triumph

Ronaldo Luís Nazário de Lima, known simply as Ronaldo, emerged from humble beginnings to become one of football's greatest strikers, earning the nickname "O Fenômeno" for his extraordinary prowess on the field. His story is a saga of resilience, breathtaking talent, and an undying love for the game that saw him overcome numerous obstacles to reach the pinnacle of global football.

Born in 1976 in Bento Ribeiro, a poor suburb of Rio de Janeiro, Brazil, Ronaldo discovered his passion for football at a young age. The streets of his neighborhood were his first stadium, where he honed his skills and dreamed of escaping poverty. His talent was undeniable, and by the age of 16, he was already making waves on the professional stage with Cruzeiro, scoring 44 goals in 47 games which quickly caught the attention of Europe's top football clubs.

Ronaldo's European journey began with PSV Eindhoven in the Netherlands, where he showcased his trademark dribbles and goal-scoring ability. His career trajectory continued upward with moves to Barcelona and Inter Milan, where he combined pace, skill, and an incredible scoring knack to dominate Europe's premier leagues. His performances were mesmerizing, marked by his ability to outrun defenders and his almost supernatural capability to finish from any position, making him a terror for defenders around the world.

However, Ronaldo's journey was not without its hardships. His career was plagued with serious knee injuries that threatened to derail his promising path. In 1999, while at the peak of his career, Ronaldo suffered a catastrophic knee injury that saw him sidelined for months. The road to recovery was long and fraught with setbacks, but Ronaldo's determination and love for the game saw him return to the field against all odds.

In 2002, Ronaldo's resilience was rewarded on the biggest stage of all—the FIFA World Cup. Leading the Brazilian national team in Japan and South Korea, Ronaldo was the tournament's standout star, scoring eight goals, including two in the final against Germany, to help Brazil clinch its fifth World Cup title. His performance was a testament to his incredible comeback and a symbol of triumph over adversity.

Following the World Cup, Ronaldo's career saw him play for Real Madrid in the famed "Galácticos" era and later for AC Milan, before returning to Brazil to conclude his professional journey. Throughout his career, despite the challenges, Ronaldo's impact on the field remained undeniable. He was not only a prolific scorer but also a source of inspiration for teammates and fans alike, showcasing the spirit of true sportsmanship and resilience.

Off the field, Ronaldo has been involved in various charitable endeavors, using his fame to improve social conditions for children in Brazil and around the world. He has also taken roles within the sport's administration, working to give back to the football community that raised him.

    Ronaldo Nazário's legacy is one of a true fighter—someone who battled through personal and professional challenges to leave an indelible mark on football. His story teaches us about the power of resilience, the importance of never giving up on your dreams, and the impact of returning love to the game that made him a global icon.

What Did We Learn from Ronaldo Nazário?

Ronaldo Nazário, known as "O Fenômeno," left an indelible mark on the world of football, embodying the essence of resilience, excellence, and the transformative power of determination. His journey from the streets of Rio de Janeiro to the pinnacle of world football is filled with lessons that extend far beyond the sports arena.

From Ronaldo, we learned the profound impact of resilience. His career was marked by spectacular highs and challenging lows, particularly his battles with severe knee injuries that could have ended his playing days. Yet, Ronaldo's remarkable comebacks—most notably his triumphant return in the 2002 World Cup—teach us that with perseverance and hard work, one can overcome almost any setback. His resilience serves as a powerful reminder that the human spirit is capable of facing tremendous adversity and emerging stronger.

We also learned about the importance of raw talent and the dedication needed to hone it. Ronaldo's natural ability was evident from a young age, but it was his dedication to improving his skills that made him a standout player. His career exemplifies how talent alone is not enough; it must be coupled with hard work and continuous improvement to reach and sustain success at the highest levels.

Ronaldo's approach to the game also highlighted the value of joy and passion in one's pursuits. Even in the face of intense pressure and expectations, he played with a sense of joy that was infectious. His smile and love for the game reminded everyone that at its heart, football is a source of happiness and inspiration, reinforcing that passion is a crucial component of success.

Additionally, Ronaldo taught us about the importance of adaptability. Throughout his career, he adapted his style of play to accommodate the changes in his physical condition and the evolution of the game itself. This ability to adapt and evolve is crucial in any long-term career, demonstrating that flexibility and openness to change are essential for longevity and continued relevance.

Finally, Ronaldo's life off the field, involving various charitable works and contributions to football administration, shows the importance of giving back. His ongoing commitment to using his platform for the betterment of others underscores the role of personal success in contributing to broader community and societal benefits.

From Ronaldo Nazário, we learn that talent, resilience, joy, adaptability, and a commitment to giving back are not just qualities of a great athlete but are attributes that can guide anyone in achieving excellence and making a positive impact in their world.

Michel Platini: Artistry, Leadership, and Legacy

Michel Platini's journey in football is a story of vision, finesse, and indelible impact, both on the field and in football administration. Born in 1955 in Jœuf, France, Platini grew up in a football-loving family, which nurtured his early passion and skill for the game. His father was a director at a local football club, which provided the perfect environment for young Platini to develop his talents.

Platini's professional career began at AS Nancy in 1972, where he quickly made a name for himself with his precise passing, strategic vision, and free-kick mastery. His skills not only revitalized his club but also earned him a move to Saint-Étienne, one of

France's premier clubs at the time. Here, Platini's flair and leadership on the pitch led to national league success and a memorable run in the European Cup.

However, it was his transfer to Juventus in 1982 that marked the peak of Platini's club career. At Juventus, he transformed into a global football icon, leading the club to numerous victories, including the 1985 European Cup. During his time in Italy, Platini was thrice awarded the Ballon d'Or, recognizing him as the best player in the world. His style of play—intelligent, elegant, and decisive—made him a favorite among fans and a respected figure among peers.

On the international stage, Platini captained the French national team to great success. His leadership culminated in winning the 1984 UEFA European Championship, where his nine goals in just five games remain a record. Platini's performance in this tournament is considered one of the finest in international football, showcasing his ability to perform at the highest level under intense pressure.

Beyond his playing days, Platini ventured into football administration, serving as the coach of the French national team and later as a key administrator in UEFA. As the president of UEFA, Platini was instrumental in initiating reforms like the Financial Fair Play regulations aimed at ensuring financial fairness among clubs. His tenure also saw the expansion of the European Championships to include more nations, broadening the scope and inclusivity of the tournament.

Platini's legacy in football is multifaceted. As a player, he was known for his artistic approach to the game, blending technical skill with strategic acumen. Off the field, his contributions to football governance have had a lasting impact on the sport's development in Europe and beyond.

Michel Platini's story teaches us about the power of vision and creativity, both in play and in leadership. It highlights the importance of adapting skills and passions to new challenges, whether on the pitch or in the boardroom. His journey is a testament to the profound influence one individual can have on the world's most popular sport, inspiring future generations to approach football—and life—with the same commitment to excellence and innovation.

What Did We Learn from Michel Platini?

Michel Platini's illustrious career as both a player and an administrator in football offers valuable lessons about skill, vision, and leadership. His journey from a local club player to a world-renowned football icon and influential administrator highlights several key attributes contributing to success in any field.

From Platini, we learned the importance of technical mastery and innovation. As a player, Platini was known for his exceptional skill, particularly his precision in passing and free-kick execution. His ability to read the game and make decisive plays demonstrated the power of having a deep understanding of one's craft. Platini's playing style emphasized creativity and intelligence, teaching us that innovation within one's role can redefine standards and elevate performance.

Leadership is another significant lesson from Platini's career. As the French national team captain, he led by example, guiding France to its first major international victory in the 1984 UEFA European Championship. His leadership style was marked by both inspiration and strategy, showing that effective leaders motivate their teams and think critically and tactically to achieve goals.

Platini also exemplified the impact of transitioning skills to new roles. After he retired from playing, he successfully shifted into administration, where he implemented significant changes in UEFA. This transition underscores the versatility of skills like strategic thinking and vision, which are valuable across various contexts. It teaches us that the skills we develop in one area can be adapted and applied to new challenges, enhancing career longevity and relevance.

Furthermore, Platini's administrative career highlighted the importance of ethical responsibility and transparency in leadership roles. His initiatives aimed at improving financial fairness among clubs and expanding the accessibility of European championships reflect a commitment to improving the sport's integrity and inclusiveness.

Lastly, Platini's story teaches us about the consequences of decisions in positions of power. His tenure as an administrator had its controversies, reminding us that leadership is subject to scrutiny, and ethical dilemmas must be navigated carefully.

From Michel Platini, we learn that excellence in performance, visionary leadership, adaptability in career roles, and ethical governance are crucial for lasting impact and legacy. His journey offers insights into transforming personal success into broader contributions, shaping industries, and influencing future generations.

George Best: Talent, Triumph, and Tragedy

George Best's story encapsulates the raw beauty and complexity of immense talent, embodying the highs of footballing brilliance and the struggles that sometimes accompany genius. Born in 1946 in Belfast, Northern Ireland, Best was discovered by a scout for Manchester United at the tender age of 15. His journey from the cobbled streets of Belfast to the lush pitches of the English Football League is a tale of meteoric rise, marked by moments of sheer brilliance that secured his place as one of the sport's all-time greats.

Best made his debut for Manchester United in 1963, and his impact was immediate and profound. With dazzling dribbling skills, extraordinary balance, and a natural flair for the game, he became an iconic figure, not just at United but across the footballing world. Best's style of play was ahead of its time; he combined technical precision with audacious creativity, making him a nightmare for defenders and a delight for spectators.

During his time at Manchester United, Best achieved tremendous success, including winning the European Cup in 1968. His performance in the European Cup final, where he scored a crucial goal, showcased his unique ability to perform at the highest levels under pressure. That same year, he was awarded the Ballon d'Or, affirming his status as one of the world's best players.

Off the field, George Best became one of football's first celebrities, known as much for his glamorous lifestyle as his footballing prowess. His charm and good looks made headlines, but the pressure of fame also led him down a path of excessive drinking and personal difficulties. Despite his struggles, Best's love for the game never waned, and his natural talent continued to shine through, although inconsistently, due to his off-field issues.

George Best's career declined in the late 1970s as his lifestyle caught up with him, leading to premature retirement. Despite his battles, Best's legacy in football remains untarnished. He is remembered for his electrifying performances, his incredible skill, and his ability to entertain and inspire football fans around the world.

Beyond the pitch, George Best's story is a poignant reminder of the pressures that can accompany talent and fame. His life teaches us about the importance of managing success and the challenges that can accompany gifted individuals. Despite his struggles, Best is celebrated as a footballer who brought joy and beauty to the sport, a true artist whose legacy continues to influence and inspire.

George Best's journey is not just a football story; it's a human story that resonates beyond the sport. It reminds us of the fleeting nature of fame and the enduring impact of genuine talent. His name remains synonymous with creativity and flair, a testament to a player who, at his best, was truly the best.

What Did We Learn from George Best?

George Best's remarkable journey through the world of football teaches us about the dazzling heights of talent and the personal challenges that can accompany it. His story is a poignant lesson in the duality of success and the human aspects of sporting brilliance.

Talent and creativity are the first lessons we learn from George Best. Known for his extraordinary skills, Best demonstrated that football is not just a game of physical prowess but also one of artistry and imagination. His ability to dribble past multiple defenders and score from improbable positions reminded us that individual creativity can change games, influence tactics, and inspire fans and players alike.

From Best, we also learned about the impact of fame on personal life. His meteoric rise to stardom brought immense pressure, illustrating how difficult it can be to manage success, especially when it arrives early. Best's experiences highlight the need for support systems and guidance for young talents rising in any high-pressure field. His life underscores the importance of mental health and well-being, aspects often overshadowed by professional accomplishments.

Resilience is another critical lesson from Best's life. Despite numerous personal and professional setbacks, including his struggles with alcoholism and the subsequent impact on his career, Best's love for the game and his innate joy when playing were evident. This resilience shows that while adversity can diminish even the brightest stars, the spirit of true passion can endure.

Additionally, George Best taught us about the consequences of lifestyle choices. His story serves as a cautionary tale about how personal decisions can affect professional life and legacy. It emphasizes the importance of discipline and moderation, qualities essential for long-term success and stability.

Lastly, George Best's legacy teaches us about the enduring nature of talent. Despite the challenges and the untimely decline of his career, Best is remembered and revered for his unmatched skills and the joy he brought to football. His story is a powerful reminder that while personal struggles may influence one's trajectory, the impact of genuine talent and moments of brilliance can leave a lasting legacy.

George Best's life, filled with both spectacular football and significant challenges, offers profound insights into the complexities of sports and fame, reminding us of the importance of balance, support, and the enduring power of human spirit and creativity.

Bobby Charlton: A Tale of Triumph and Tenacity

Sir Bobby Charlton's journey through football is not only a story of sporting excellence but also one of survival, resilience, and commitment. Born in 1937 in Ashington, England, Charlton grew up in a football-loving family and was quickly recognized for his prodigious talent. His career, marked by both collective success and personal trials, has become a beacon of inspiration in the world of sports.

Charlton joined Manchester United in 1953, and his rise was meteoric. Known for his powerful shooting, precision passing, and strategic intelligence, he became a key player under the management of Sir Matt Busby. His early years at United were marked by promise and success, culminating in winning the league title in 1957.

However, his career—and life—took a dramatic turn on February 6, 1958. Charlton survived the Munich air disaster, which claimed the lives of 23 people, including eight of his Manchester United teammates. The tragedy deeply affected Charlton, but it also showcased his remarkable resilience. He not only returned to play for Manchester United but also became a cornerstone in rebuilding the team, later known as the "Busby Babes."

Charlton's leadership and formidable skills on the pitch led to a resurgence of Manchester United. His contributions were pivotal in helping the club secure the English Football League title in 1965 and again in

1967. His greatest club achievement came in 1968 when Manchester United won the European Cup—Charlton scored two goals in the final against Benfica, ensuring a 4-1 victory that marked the first time an English club had won the competition.

On the international stage, Charlton's legacy is equally significant. He was instrumental in England's 1966 FIFA World Cup victory on home soil. His performances throughout the tournament were outstanding, culminating in a win against West Germany in the final, a victory that remains England's only World Cup title to date.

Off the field, Charlton's gentlemanly demeanor, sportsmanship, and dedication to football have made him a revered figure.

After retiring as a player, he continued to contribute to the sport, taking on managerial roles and later becoming a director at Manchester United. He has also been involved in various charitable endeavors, further solidifying his role as an ambassador for the game.

Bobby Charlton's story is a poignant reminder of the power of perseverance and the human capacity to overcome adversity. His career, marked by exceptional achievements and underscored by his recovery from personal tragedy, teaches us that with determination and spirit, one can transcend difficulties and achieve greatness. Sir Bobby Charlton not only left a mark on football with his skills and accomplishments but also with his resilience, leadership, and integrity, embodying the true spirit of the sport.

What Did We Learn from Bobby Charlton?

Bobby Charlton's illustrious career and life story offer profound lessons about resilience, leadership, and the enduring spirit of sportsmanship, making him a true icon of football.

From Charlton, we learned the incredible power of resilience. His survival of the Munich air disaster and his subsequent return to top-level football is a testament to human fortitude. Despite experiencing immense personal loss and trauma, Charlton not only continued to play but also helped rebuild his team and led them to new heights. His journey teaches us that adversity can be met with strength and can serve as a catalyst for profound personal and collective achievements.

Leadership by example is another crucial lesson from Charlton's life. Throughout his career at Manchester United and on the international stage with England, Charlton demonstrated what it means to lead with humility and dedication. His ability to inspire his teammates, coupled with his outstanding personal performances, particularly during critical moments like the 1966 World Cup and the 1968 European Cup, shows the impact of leading not just with words, but with actions.

Charlton also exemplified the virtue of sportsmanship. Known for his fair play and respect for opponents, he was a gentleman both on and off the pitch. In an era when football was becoming highly competitive and sometimes harsh, Charlton maintained high standards of conduct, reminding us that how one plays the game is as important as the outcome.

Moreover, we learned from Charlton the importance of contributing to one's community and sport. After retiring from professional play, he didn't leave the world of football; instead, he continued to serve in various capacities, including coaching and management and engaging in charity work. This ongoing commitment underscores the idea that one's influence and responsibility do not end with retirement but evolve to include mentoring the next generation and giving back to the community.

Finally, Charlton's life teaches us about the endurance of legacy. Through his achievements and how he conducted his life, he set a benchmark for future generations. His legacy in football is not just built on the records and titles he earned but also on the respect he garnered and the inspiration he continues to provide to players and fans alike.

From Bobby Charlton, we learn that greatness encompasses more than just skill and achievements; it includes resilience, leadership, sportsmanship, community involvement, and the ability to inspire and elevate those around us. His life is a blueprint for not just aspiring sportspeople but anyone looking to overcome challenges and lead with integrity.

Alfredo Di Stefano: The Blond Arrow Who Transformed Real Madrid

Alfredo Di Stefano's story is not just one of personal triumph but also a profound impact on one of the world's most iconic football clubs, Real Madrid. Born in 1926 in Buenos Aires, Argentina, Di Stefano grew up in a country passionate about football, which shaped his early career. His journey from the gritty neighborhoods of Buenos Aires to the grandeur of Madrid is a testament to his relentless pursuit of excellence and his transformative influence on the sport.

Di Stefano began his professional career in Argentina with River Plate, one of the country's top clubs, where he quickly made a name for himself as a formidable forward. His career took him to Colombia before finally landing in Spain, where he would make his indelible mark. In 1953, he joined Real Madrid, a club that, at the time, had not achieved the same level of success as its fiercer rivals, including Barcelona.

At Real Madrid, Di Stefano became the catalyst for change. His arrival coincided with one of the most successful eras in the club's history. Known as "La Saeta Rubia" (The Blond Arrow), Di Stefano was famed for his powerful playing style, incredible stamina, and versatile abilities. He wasn't just a forward; he could play almost anywhere on the pitch, influencing the game in ways few others could.

Under Di Stefano's leadership, Real Madrid won an astonishing five consecutive European Cups from 1956 to 1960, a record that stands as one of the greatest achievements in club football. Di Stefano himself scored in each of these five finals, showcasing his knack for performing in critical moments. His role in the 7-3 victory over Eintracht Frankfurt in the 1960 European Cup final remains one of the most celebrated performances in the history of the sport.

Di Stefano's influence extended beyond his goal-scoring. He shaped the playing style and tactics of Real Madrid, embedding a high-intensity, attacking philosophy that would become a hallmark of the club. His ability to read the game and his relentless pursuit of victory inspired his teammates and intimidated his opponents.

Beyond the pitch, Di Stefano also left a legacy of internationalism in football. Holding citizenship in Argentina, Colombia, and Spain, and having played in all three countries, he broke traditional boundaries and set a precedent for the global nature of the sport.

After retiring from playing, Di Stefano didn't stray far from football or Real Madrid. He managed several clubs, including Real Madrid, and continued to influence the sport through his strategic insights and profound understanding of the game.

Alfredo Di Stefano's story teaches us that true greatness often requires not only individual excellence but also the ability to uplift and transform those around you. His contributions to Real Madrid and football at large demonstrate how one person's talents and vision can reshape an institution's destiny. Di Stefano is not just a football legend; he is a symbol of how enduring impact is achieved through a combination of skill, leadership, and transformative vision

What Did We Learn from Alfredo Di Stefano?

Alfredo Di Stefano's remarkable career offers profound lessons about versatility, leadership, and the power of transformative influence in sports and beyond.

Versatility is one of the primary lessons from Di Stefano's playing style. Known as "La Saeta Rubia" (The Blond Arrow), he was celebrated not just for his ability to score but for his effectiveness in virtually any position on the field. This adaptability made him an invaluable asset to Real Madrid and serves as a lesson in the importance of flexibility and broad skill sets in achieving success.

From Di Stefano, we also learned the essence of leadership. His presence on the field was more than just physical; he was a strategic leader who could elevate the performance of his entire team. Di Stefano's ability to lead by example, coupled with his understanding of the game, helped forge Real Madrid into one of the most formidable teams in the world. His style of leadership reminds us that true leaders inspire others to reach greater heights.

Di Stefano's career exemplified professional excellence. His relentless pursuit of victory and continuous improvement set standards in football that influenced generations. His commitment to excellence in every match, whether a local league game or a European Cup final, teaches us the value of consistency and high standards in one's profession.

Additionally, Di Stefano taught us about the impact of cultural integration in sports. As an Argentine playing in Spain, and with prior stints in Colombia, Di Stefano broke national boundaries and became a global icon in football. His international career path highlights the benefits of embracing different cultures and perspectives, enriching both the individual and the teams he was part of.

Lastly, the career of Alfredo Di Stefano underscores the transformative power of influential individuals. Through his impact at Real Madrid, Di Stefano not only helped the club achieve unprecedented success but also helped shape its identity and philosophy, effects that are still evident today. His influence teaches us that one individual's abilities and vision can leave a lasting legacy on an institution.

From Alfredo Di Stefano, we learn that versatility, leadership, a commitment to excellence, cultural adaptability, and transformative influence are not just qualities of a great athlete but are attributes that can guide anyone in achieving enduring success and impact in their endeavors.

Gerd Müller: The Goal-Scoring Machine

Gerd Müller's story is a testament to sheer talent, determination, and an uncanny ability to find the back of the net, earning him the nickname "Der Bomber." Born in 1945 in Nördlingen, Germany, Müller rose from modest beginnings to become one of football's greatest strikers, setting records that stood for decades.

Müller began his professional career at TSV 1861 Nördlingen, but it was at Bayern Munich where he truly made his mark. Joining in 1964 when Bayern was still in the regional league, his prolific goal-scoring helped the club ascend to the Bundesliga and subsequently dominate German football. Müller wasn't physically imposing—standing just 5 feet 9 inches tall and with a stocky build—but his agility, acceleration, and instinctive positioning made him a formidable forward.

Throughout his career, Müller scored an astonishing 365 goals in 427 Bundesliga games, a record that remained unbroken for over 40 years. His scoring prowess was not limited to domestic competitions; he also left his mark on the international stage. Müller was instrumental in West Germany's 1972 European Championship win and the 1974 World Cup victory on home soil. In the 1970 World Cup, he was the tournament's top scorer with 10 goals, showcasing his ability to perform against the world's best.

Müller's style was characterized by quick reactions and a one-track mind toward the goal. His ability to anticipate where the ball would end up and his quick feet in tight spaces made him nearly unstoppable in the box. His record of 40 goals in a single Bundesliga season in 1971-72 stood until 2021, underscoring his exceptional skills as a finisher.

Off the field, Müller's life was not without challenges. Post-retirement, he struggled with alcoholism and depression, battles that he later overcame with the support of his family and Bayern Munich, the club that remained loyal to him beyond his playing days. Recognizing his struggles, Bayern Munich helped him find treatment and later provided him with a coaching role for their youth teams, allowing him to give back to the game that had given him so much.

Gerd Müller's legacy is profound. He redefined the role of a striker with his incredible scoring record and efficiency. His life teaches us about the power of resilience, both in terms of a career punctuated by goal-scoring records and in his personal life, facing and overcoming post-career challenges. Müller is remembered not only for his on-field achievements but also for his character and the courage with which he faced life's difficulties. His story is a powerful reminder that success often comes with its own set of challenges, and how one handles these challenges can define one's legacy as much as any professional accomplishment.

What Did We Learn from Gerd Müller?

Gerd Müller, known as "Der Bomber," left an indelible mark on football with his remarkable goal-scoring abilities and his journey, from which we can draw several valuable lessons.

Maximizing One's Talents: Müller was not the most physically imposing player, nor was he the fastest. Yet, he mastered the art of goal-scoring with uncanny positioning and lethal finishing. From Müller, we learned that excelling is not about having all the best attributes but maximizing your strengths. His ability to find spaces in the defense and anticipate the ball's movement allowed him to outscore taller, faster defenders consistently. This teaches us the importance of recognizing and cultivating our unique strengths to achieve success.

Resilience in the Face of Challenges: Müller's story is also a powerful lesson in resilience. Despite facing challenges towards the end of his playing career and post-retirement, including struggles with alcoholism and depression, Müller's journey through recovery, supported by his family and club, shows the strength it takes to ask for help and the importance of community support in overcoming personal battles.

Impact of Humility and Work Ethic: Müller's humility and work ethic were as legendary as his scoring record. He remained a down-to-earth, approachable individual despite his superstar status, endearing him to fans and teammates alike. His dedication to improving his craft, even after achieving top honors in football, underscores the value of ongoing hard work and humility in maintaining success and personal growth.

Giving Back to the Sport: After overcoming his challenges, Müller dedicated part of his life to coaching, particularly focusing on young players at Bayern Munich. This transition from a world-class player to a mentor for the next generation highlights the importance of giving back to one's community or field and sharing the lessons and experiences gained to help others grow and succeed.

Legacy and Recognition: Finally, Müller's legacy in football, marked by record-setting performances and key victories, teaches us that true greatness often leaves a lasting impact, inspiring future generations. His story reminds us that achievements can transcend personal accolades and become benchmarks that motivate and elevate the entire sport.

From Gerd Müller, we learn about the profound impacts of maximizing talents, resilience, humility, and the importance of contributing positively to the community—lessons that are applicable far beyond the world of sports.

Paolo Maldini: A Legacy of Excellence and Loyalty

Paolo Maldini, a name synonymous with defensive mastery and unwavering loyalty, stands as one of the greatest defenders in the history of football. Born in 1968 in Milan, Italy, Maldini was destined for football greatness, being the son of Cesare Maldini, a former player and later a coach. Paolo's career at AC Milan, which spanned an incredible 25 years, is a testament to his skill, dedication, and commitment to a single club.

Maldini made his debut for AC Milan in 1985 at just 16 years old and quickly became a fixture in the team. Over the years, his exceptional positioning, tactical intelligence, and ability to read the game made him one of the most formidable defenders in the world. Maldini wasn't just a defensive stalwart; he was also a leader on the pitch, eventually captaining Milan and the Italian national team.

   Throughout his career, Maldini won numerous titles with Milan, including seven Serie A championships and five UEFA Champions League trophies. His performances in European competitions were particularly notable, highlighted by his role in Milan's back-to-back Champions League wins in 1989 and 1990 and again in 2003 and 2007. Maldini's ability to perform at the highest level in crucial matches underscored his reputation as a player who thrived under pressure.

Maldini's style of play was characterized by elegance, strength, and a profound understanding of the game. Unlike many defenders of his or any era, Maldini combined physicality with grace, making clean tackles and rarely resorting to fouls to stop his opponents. His sportsmanship and professionalism on the field were as respected as his technical abilities.

Off the field, Maldini was known for his calm demeanor and leadership qualities. He was not merely a captain by armband but a true leader who inspired his teammates through his actions and dedication. Maldini's influence extended beyond his play, shaping the careers of those around him and setting a standard of excellence at AC Milan.

After retiring in 2009, Maldini left a legacy that few can match. Notably, he rejected numerous offers from other clubs throughout his career, embodying the spirit of loyalty and commitment to his team. His farewell match was an emotional tribute to his contributions, not only to Milan but to football as a whole.

Paolo Maldini's story teaches us the value of dedication, the importance of consistency, and the impact of leading by example. His career demonstrates that true greatness requires more than just talent; it requires a commitment to excellence, a deep love for the game, and an unwavering loyalty to one's principles and team. Maldini remains not just a legend in football but a symbol of integrity and class in sports.

What Did We Learn from Paolo Maldini?

Paolo Maldini's illustrious career at AC Milan, marked by exceptional skill, leadership, and loyalty, offers timeless lessons for both the sports world and beyond.

Excellence through Consistency and Hard Work: Maldini's career exemplifies how consistency and dedication are fundamental to achieving and maintaining high standards. Known for his disciplined training regimen and commitment to continuous improvement, Maldini showed that sustaining peak performance over a long career requires relentless hard work and dedication to craft.

Leadership by Example: As a captain of both AC Milan and the Italian national team,

Maldini demonstrated that true leadership is about setting an example with one's actions. His ability to stay composed under pressure, make decisive plays, and maintain high-performance standards inspired his teammates to elevate their games. Maldini's leadership style teaches us that the most influential leaders are those who lead by example, showing the way forward through their actions rather than just words.

Loyalty and Integrity: In an era when players frequently transfer between clubs, Maldini's unwavering loyalty to AC Milan stands out. He spent his entire 25-year career with the club, rejecting offers from other teams. This loyalty not only earned him the respect of his peers and fans but also demonstrated his deep commitment to the values of integrity and loyalty, rare in modern professional sports.

Sportsmanship and Fair Play: Maldini was renowned for his clean style of play. Despite being a defender, where physical and sometimes rough tactics are common, he was noted for his ability to make clean tackles and his respect for opponents. His career is a testament to the fact that one can be competitive and successful while still upholding the highest standards of sportsmanship.

Influence Beyond the Field: Paolo Maldini's impact on football continued even after his retirement, demonstrating that a player's influence extends beyond just their time on the pitch. By setting a standard of excellence, professionalism, and integrity, he has left a legacy that influences not only current players but also future generations who look to him as a model of what a sportsman should be.

From Paolo Maldini, we learn that lasting success is built on a foundation of hard work, leadership, loyalty, and integrity. His career teaches us that these values are just as important as talent and can define a legacy as much as victories and titles.

www.ingramcontent.com/pod-product-compliance
Lightning Source LLC
Chambersburg PA
CBHW072210070526
44585CB00015B/1277